D1524588

Less Is More

JOIN THE LOW-WASTE MOVEMENT

LEAH PAYNE

WITHDRAWN

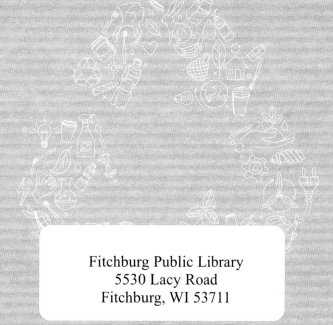

Fitchburg Public Library
5530 Lacy Road
Fitchburg, WI 53711

ORCA BOOK PUBLISHERS

Text copyright © Leah Payne 2023

Published in Canada and the United States in 2023 by Orca Book Publishers.
orcabook.com

All rights reserved. No part of this publication may be reproduced
or transmitted in any form or by any means, electronic or
mechanical, including photocopying, recording or by any
information storage and retrieval system now known or to be
invented, without permission in writing from the publisher.

Library and Archives Canada Cataloguing in Publication
Title: Less is more : join the low-waste movement / Leah Payne.
Names: Payne, Leah (Leah S.), author.
Series: Orca footprints.
Description: Series statement: Orca footprints ; 28 |
Includes bibliographical references and index.
Identifiers: Canadiana (print) 20220480559 |
Canadiana (ebook) 20220480583 | ISBN 9781459835443 (hardcover) |
ISBN 9781459835450 (PDF) | ISBN 9781459835467 (EPUB)
Subjects: LCSH: Waste minimization—Juvenile literature. |
LCSH: Sustainable living—Juvenile literature.
Classification: LCC TD793.9 .P39 2023 | DDC j363.73/7—dc23

Library of Congress Control Number: 2022950242

Summary: Part of the nonfiction Orca Footprints series for middle-
grade readers, this book explores the low-waste movement and how
kids can get involved. Illustrated with photographs throughout.

Orca Book Publishers is committed to reducing the consumption of
nonrenewable resources in the production of our books. We make
every effort to use materials that support a sustainable future.

Orca Book Publishers gratefully acknowledges the support for
its publishing programs provided by the following agencies:
the Government of Canada, the Canada Council for the
Arts and the Province of British Columbia through the BC
Arts Council and the Book Publishing Tax Credit.

The author and publisher have made every effort to ensure that the
information in this book was correct at the time of publication. The
author and publisher do not assume any liability for any loss, damage,
or disruption caused by errors or omissions. Every effort has been
made to trace copyright holders and to obtain their permission for the
use of copyrighted material. The publisher apologizes for any errors
or omissions and would be grateful if notified of any corrections that
should be incorporated in future reprints or editions of this book.

Front cover photos by SolStock/Getty Images and
Mayur Kakade/Getty Images
Back cover photos by dragana991/Getty Images,
monkeybusinessimages/Getty Images and Elva Etienne/Getty Images
Author photo by Notting Hill Photography
Design by Jenn Playford
Edited by Kirstie Hudson

Printed and bound in South Korea.

26 25 24 23 • 1 2 3 4

JURGITA VAICIKEVICIENE / EYEEM/GETTY IMAGES

For my son. You inspire me every day to keep fighting for the health of our shared planet.

Contents

CHAPTER ONE
WHAT'S THE DEAL WITH WASTE?

CHAPTER TWO
NO, THANKS! AVOID AND REDUCE

CHAPTER THREE
LET'S GET CREATIVE: REUSE

CHAPTER FOUR
ALL'S WELL THAT ENDS WELL: RECYCLE AND ROT

Introduction

Do you and your family try to shop in a low-waste way? Buying products without packaging is one great way to help reduce waste. NATALIADERIABINA/GETTY IMAGES

What comes to mind when you think of garbage? If you think "stinky" or "smelly," you wouldn't be wrong! But what about "pollution" or *"zero waste"*? Maybe you've heard the reports of the Great Pacific Garbage Patch swirling in the ocean. Maybe you've seen the heartbreaking photos of whales and seabirds with trash in their bellies. Or maybe you've heard the statistic that only 9 percent of our plastic waste actually gets recycled (yikes, I know).

If you find these issues hard to read about, know that you're not alone. I do too, and so do tons of other people around the world. The great news is that we can make a difference through our eco-friendly actions and activism. Over the past few years, living in a low-waste way has become easier than ever—and even (dare I say it?) cool! In my own low-waste journey, I learned that some strategies work for me and my family, like using simple *visible mending* techniques to extend the life span of my family's clothes. But some strategies didn't work for us, like making every meal from scratch to cut down on food packaging. Some things may not work for you, like if you live in a rural area that doesn't have **refill** stores or curbside recycling pickup. That's totally fine. Everyone's eco-friendly strategies will be unique to them. Yours will be unique to you too.

That's why this book is focused on solutions for individuals—simple actions for your everyday life. In the following chapters we'll use the **waste hierarchy** to guide us in our efforts to avoid, reduce, reuse, recycle and rot. You'll read about things you can do to reduce your own waste, and also how to take action in your community. We'll also meet some inspiring young people who are working to reduce waste in their homes, schools and communities. Ready? Let's go!

We can all work as a team to help keep litter out of the environment.
ZORAN ZEREMSKI/SHUTTERSTOCK.COM

Many people buy bulk food—like pasta—in lightweight bags and then transfer it to larger containers when they get home. Clear glass containers are great because you can see exactly how much you have. MONKEYBUSINESSIMAGES/GETTY IMAGES

CHAPTER ONE

What's the Deal with Waste?

What is waste anyway? And what does it mean to live in a low-waste way? In this chapter we'll answer those questions and look at some of the problems too, like where our garbage goes and why our society can do a whole lot better at managing its (so-called) waste.

WASTE: LET'S MAKE THE INVISIBLE VISIBLE!

You know the expression "one person's trash is another person's treasure"? That's a pretty good way to define trash. Trash is only trash because we decide to (you guessed it!) trash it. What we end up throwing "away" depends on many other things—for example, society's deciding it's "disposable" rather than "reusable," whether we have recycling or composting facilities in our area or whether we can think of a creative way to repurpose it.

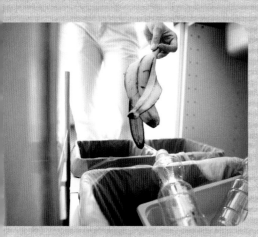

Where do food scraps go after you're finished with them? Rather than throwing them into a plastic garbage bag, consider composting instead. ALEKSANDRA SUZI/SHUTTERSTOCK.COM

As a society, we use (and dispose of) so much plastic! It might not seem that way when we look at just our own household garbage and recycling, but when everyone's is added up, the amount is pretty mind-boggling.

FG TRADE/GETTY IMAGES

In fact, it takes some creative thinking to even *see* waste in the first place. Most of us are so used to waste that we don't really notice it. For example, imagine standing in your grocery store's produce section. Do you grab a plastic produce bag to hold your oranges? Next time you're at the store, consider seeing this plastic bag as waste, and ask your family to do so too. The more critically we observe our environment, the more we can take action and make things better.

WHY DO WE WASTE SO MUCH?

We create way too much waste in North America. It started ramping up after World War II, when people were encouraged to shop and consume more to help boost the economy. Many factories transitioned from building things needed for the war to building things for people to buy. New technologies—like plastics—also became much more common.

Does your local grocery store carry a good selection of unpackaged produce? If not, consider asking the produce manager if they can bring in more unpackaged options.

MAKIKO TANIGAWA/GETTY IMAGES

People who are members of underrepresented communities, such as Black, Indigenous or other racialized groups, are more likely to live closer to toxic-waste facilities, like factories, landfills and dumps. Sadly, the people in these communities often suffer health problems. This is one example of *environmental racism*.

Plastic didn't always fill our homes—it's a relatively recent phenomenon. This ad from 1952 marketed plastic products to women for use in the kitchen.

F8 ARCHIVE/ALAMY STOCK PHOTO

Plastics (and other materials) have some pretty amazing qualities and come in handy for lots of different things. Unfortunately, more plastics plus more shopping equals more **resources** used, and more waste and pollution created. Although people were becoming pretty good at manufacturing plastics, they hadn't yet figured out how to dispose of them properly. It wasn't until the 1970s that the first plastic recycling mill was built in Pennsylvania. Recycling is helpful, but it's not a perfect solution. Even today, only 9 percent of plastic around the world is recycled.

DISPOSABLE COFFEE CUPS

The rate of plastic production has continued to increase since the post-war days and has grown faster than that of any other material since the 1970s. Today, sadly, **industrialized** countries continue to take and use up more than their fair share of the earth's resources to make things such as plastic. According to the United Nations Environmental Program, humans now produce about 441 million tons (400 million metric tons) of plastic waste per year. A significant portion of the waste comes from convenience items such as disposable cutlery and coffee cups. There's much more than we can dispose of or reuse in a way that's environmentally friendly. All in all, our on-the-go **consumerist** society is bad news for our shared planet. We need to be mindful of how much we use *and* what happens to it after we use it.

It's important to remember that it doesn't have to be this way. Creating this much waste is a relatively new practice for us humans. For thousands of years, people lived in a naturally low-waste way, or even no-waste way, and many of those practices continue today. Musqueam people return salmon carcasses to rivers after eating the salmon. This practice helps boost nutrient levels in the water. Indigenous Peoples in West Africa have used "waste" such as ash to help make soil fertile and healthy. At the beginning of this chapter we asked what waste really is.

Here, we can see that so-called waste is used in valuable ways. Indigenous communities talk about life as a balance. If something can't be used right away it is respectfully returned to the earth to become part of the cycle again.

WHERE DOES OUR WASTE GO?

When we throw something away, where does it go? Here are a few different places that it can end up.

- Recycling: Items that are recycled are collected by local programs and then sent to and processed by any number of other companies. These companies could be in your community or even overseas. Your old paper, for example, could end up as an egg carton in its next life.
- *Compost*: Organic material like food scraps can be composted, either by people at home or by municipal green-waste programs. Composting is a natural process that turns this organic material into nutrient-rich soil.
- *Landfills*: Landfills are where most of our garbage is meant to end up when we throw it, well, in the garbage bin. Many people think landfills are just big piles of garbage, but they're actually carefully managed places. For example, care must be taken to make sure garbage doesn't seep into the ground or nearby **waterways**, contaminating it. Decomposing material in landfills can emit a powerful **greenhouse gas** called methane, which contributes to climate change. This is different than the natural decomposition that occurs with compost.
- In our environment, as pollution on land and in the water: Unfortunately our garbage doesn't always end up where it belongs. Whether it happens on purpose (like when people litter) or by accident (like when items get blown off garbage trucks on the way to landfills), garbage can pollute our environment and cause lots of problems.

Have you ever visited a landfill? Some offer tours to students. Ask your teacher if your class can go on a field trip to a local landfill to learn how your city manages its waste.
VCHAL/GETTY IMAGES

In 2021 an estimated 3.4 billion single-use face masks or shields were discarded every day worldwide due to the COVID-19 pandemic. Although medical equipment is necessary and important, it's also important that we dispose of it responsibly and keep it out of the environment.

The problem isn't just that most garbage doesn't decompose for years. Garbage, like plastic waste, can also harm animals that eat it thinking it is food or become trapped (entangled) in it. Plastic even contaminates the world's water with tiny particles called **microplastics** that animals—including humans—drink.

We never really know if our garbage and recycling will end up in the right place. That's why it's so important to reduce the waste we create in the first place—and help others reduce their waste too!

(ALMOST) NO GARBAGE

All around the world we can find people who are trying to reduce the amount of waste created at home, school and work. Many businesses, communities and governments are also trying to reduce the amount of waste they create and resources they use. It's all part of the zero-waste movement. But before we dive into *how* to create less waste, it's important to clear up a few misconceptions.

Birds and other animals can quickly become tangled in plastic and other garbage. In addition to not littering, it's important that we all work to reduce waste in the first place.
TSVIBRAV/GETTY IMAGES

This plastic bag looks a bit like a jellyfish, doesn't it? That's most likely what turtles think when they eat plastic bags. An estimated 52 percent of turtles have eaten plastic waste.
RICHCAREY/GETTY IMAGES

First, you might be thinking, Is it really possible to not create any waste at all? It's true that the way our society is designed, creating *no* waste would be extremely hard to do. That's why many people prefer the term *low waste* rather than *zero waste*—it's seen as more attainable and inclusive, so we will use that term in this book too.

Also, the zero-waste movement has sometimes been criticized for seeming expensive or overly focused on aesthetics (the look of things). The truth is, we don't need to buy fancy glass containers to replace our disposable plastic ones to be considered low-waste. In fact, using what you already have in your home embodies the true spirit of reducing waste (and it saves money too)! Many cost-cutting strategies, such as meal planning and mending, are naturally low-waste.

Finally, although there may be more discussion these days about reducing our waste, as we've already learned, it's not truly a new idea at all. As we continue our own low-waste journeys, it's important to remember and learn from those who have been practicing sustainability for a very long time.

Plastic-free products can be beautiful and functional. But what's even better than buying them is using what we already have at home. Do you have a favorite reusable snack container or water bottle?
NATALIA DERIABINA/SHUTTERSTOCK.COM

Pushing for Change

And it's not just about our own daily lives. It can be easy to become focused on our individual actions, like reducing our use of plastic bags. But thinking of the big picture is even more important. Living in a low-waste way also means pushing for eco-friendly changes in our communities, schools and workplaces. For example, imagine bringing a reusable water bottle with you when you're away from home for a long time. If you didn't have anywhere to refill your water bottle, it would be hard to avoid buying bottled water. But if refill stations (specialty stations designed with taps specifically for refilling water bottles) are nearby, it's much easier to be low-waste. Plus, we can only refill our water bottles if we have access to safe, clean drinking water, which some people do not have.

Water-bottle refill stations are popping up seemingly everywhere, from schools to airports to parks. These handy stations make it easier to get clean drinking water on the go, so we can avoid buying bottled water.
LEOPATRIZI/GETTY IMAGES

It is estimated that over 50 billion disposable coffee cups are used (and thrown "away") by North Americans every year. Next time you visit your favorite café, bring your own cup—and encourage your friends to do the same!

THURTELL/GETTY IMAGES

Glass jars are a favorite of refill stores and takeback programs because they can be cleaned, sterilized and reused over and over again.

CAVAN IMAGES/GETTY IMAGES

Many Indigenous communities in Canada have long-term drinking-water advisories, meaning their tap water isn't safe to drink. In 2022 there were 34 advisories in place across the country. As of that year the Neskantaga First Nation (north of Thunder Bay, Ontario) had not had access to clean drinking water for more than 27 years.

That's why, in addition to making our own low-waste changes, it's important to make eco-friendly changes in our communities and push for change from those in power. Young people who are not yet old enough to vote can still speak out by contacting politicians, writing letters and attending local council meetings. Ask your teacher to make this a school-wide initiative!

CLOSE THE LOOP

One of the biggest, most important ways that companies and governments can reduce waste is to transition from linear to circular economies. That might sound complicated, but it's pretty straightforward.

Linear Economy

A *linear economy* is sometimes referred to as the "take–make–dispose" model. That means resources are taken from the earth, made into products and then disposed of once people are done using them. It's called a linear economy because it moves in a straight line through the various steps in the supply chain.

For example, *fossil fuels* might be extracted from the earth, processed and eventually made into plastic containers for yogurt. Then customers throw the containers in the garbage after finishing the yogurt.

Circular Economy

In a *circular economy*, waste is reduced. Strategies like *closed loop* systems focus on repurposing, repairing or reusing materials. It's a more mindful method of making goods, one that examines the life cycle of a product and its materials at every step in the supply chain. It's called a circular economy because it moves in a circular line, and resources and materials are kept within the economy for as long as possible rather than being disposed of.

For example, raw materials such as sand might be extracted from the earth, processed and eventually made into glass containers for yogurt, which customers return to the store or food company to be cleaned and reused by future customers.

Some companies have "takeback" programs where people can return their used products or product packaging to be recycled or made into other things. For example, the Native Shoes Remix Project recycles worn-out Native Shoes to create materials like playground flooring.

This watering can is made from recycled plastic. The next time you're at the store consider looking for products that are made from recycled materials. How many can you find?

DONALD TRUNG/WIKIMEDIA COMMONS/CC BY-SA 4.0

ADAPTED FROM CATHERINE WEETMAN/WIKIMEDIA COMMONS/CC BY 4.0

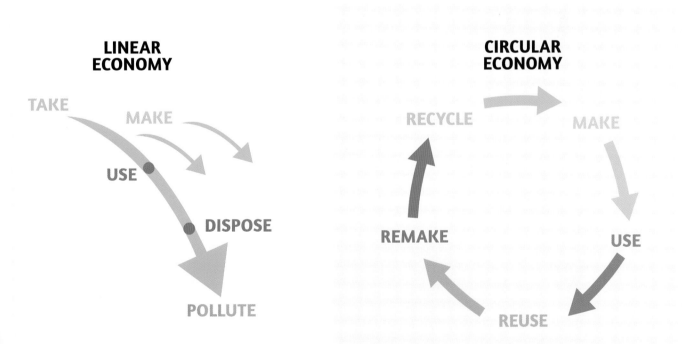

LINEAR ECONOMY

TAKE · MAKE · USE · DISPOSE · POLLUTE

CIRCULAR ECONOMY

RECYCLE · MAKE · USE · REUSE · REMAKE

THE WASTE HIERARCHY

When we're trying to reduce waste, it's helpful to follow the waste hierarchy. This is a tool that looks like an upside-down pyramid and ranks ways to use and dispose of things from most preferred to least preferred. Even though we're told to reduce, reuse and recycle, sometimes it feels like most of the emphasis gets put on recycle, even though there are more important steps we should try to follow first.

The waste hierarchy is used by lots of different groups, from businesses that are planning product design and manufacturing to individuals who are planning their grocery shopping. The waste hierarchy below is one of many different versions. Let's look at the categories as a person would rather than a business. Imagine you're heading to your favorite neighborhood café for lunch...

THE WASTE HIERARCHY

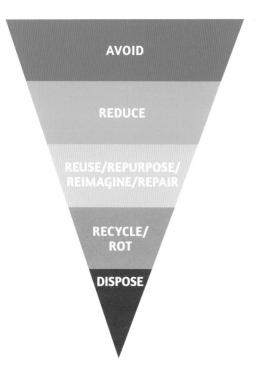

Avoid: The best way to deal with waste is to prevent it in the first place. Maybe the café has an option to eat in the restaurant. Ask to have your lunch on a reusable plate with reusable cutlery instead of in a takeaway container with plastic cutlery that will be thrown away.

Reduce: When preventing waste isn't possible, we might be able to reduce the waste we create. In our café example, this might look like saying "No, thanks!" to disposable cutlery if we need the takeout option for lunch. Instead we can bring a little "on the go" kit with us that contains things like a reusable water bottle or travel mug, cutlery or chopsticks, and a cloth napkin.

Reuse (and repurpose, reimagine and repair): Sometimes we try our best but end up with waste anyway. Maybe we could wash and reuse the plastic container from our takeout lunch for storing things at home, like arts and crafts supplies.

Recycle (and rot): We're all familiar with the concept of recycling. When we're done using (and reusing) the plastic takeout container, it's time to recycle it. Often this category also includes "rot"—composting organic matter.

Dispose: This is the least preferred option. Those who live in a low-waste way try to avoid having to send things to the landfill whenever possible. Although many things can be creatively and safely reused or recycled, some things can't. In our example, this might be a small plastic ketchup packet.

Over the next few chapters we will explore these categories in more detail, focusing on how to avoid, reduce, reuse and recycle/rot.

Interested in learning how to repair your old things, like electronics? Look for repair cafes and workshops for young people near you. Community centers, libraries and non-profit organizations often offer events and programs.
MASKOT/GETTY IMAGES

Ban the Bottle

Can an entire university stop using single-use plastic bottles? Absolutely! When Mireta Strandberg-Salmon was a high school student, she campaigned to get her school to stop selling bottled water in its vending machines. After she graduated and became a student at Simon Fraser University (SFU), she founded Ban the Bottle to help the university eliminate bottled water too. "Don't assume that the way things are is the way they have to be," Mireta says. "As young people we see the world differently than adults, and our perspective matters!"

Ban the Bottle members worked with the administration to provide green alternatives to plastic use, like refill stations all over campus. In 2021 SFU officially phased out all single-use plastic drink bottles. Through the university's Re-use for Good task force, SFU has also phased out other single-use items like plastic cutlery and straws.

Ban the Bottle's co-president Antonia Kowalewski says that activism "can spark a change around you, especially if you talk about what you're doing and create conversations around it."

Co-president Elaina Buenaventura agrees. "Everyone has a sense of power in them that they can step into," they say.

Mireta, Elaina and Antonia smile and hold their reusable water bottles during an online Ban the Bottle meeting.
BAN THE BOTTLE SFU

CHAPTER TWO

No, Thanks! Avoid and Reduce

Unpackaged and low-waste groceries like these can be purchased from specialty bulk or refill stores. But you can often find them at regular grocery stores and farmers' markets too.
ANCHIY/GETTY IMAGES

The top two, and most important, steps of the waste hierarchy are avoid and reduce. This chapter will arm you with some great tips and strategies for preventing waste in the first place. Get ready to say, "No, thanks!"

TIME FOR A WASTE AUDIT

Time to roll up your sleeves! A *waste audit* is a fantastic (and fun) way to figure out exactly what types of waste you and your family create and then come up with a plan to help avoid and reduce it in the future.

Safety first! Only do this activity with parental supervision. Some household waste may be dangerous to handle, like the sharp edges of opened food cans, batteries or used face masks. Go slowly and carefully, and wear gloves.

When you do a waste audit, you might be surprised at what sorts of items are the most common in your household waste. Channel your inner scientist by creating a tally, graph, pie chart or other visual way to assess what you find. IMGORTHAND/GETTY IMAGES

Here's what you do:

1. Gather everyone in your household, if possible.
2. Collect your household garbage and recycling bins, a pencil or pen and a notebook.
3. Here's the fun—and messy!—part. Dump the bins out one by one (use some newspaper, an old towel or a tarp to keep the floor clean).
4. Ask yourselves, What kind of waste is inside? Is there a lot of a certain type? Write it down.
5. Ask yourselves, Is there any way to reduce this waste in the future? Perhaps you can help your family make different choices or come up with some creative solutions and DIY projects at home.
6. Reassess at a later date. You can do this activity again in a few weeks to see the progress you've made!

An estimated 20 percent of online purchases are returned, which can create more waste. Returned items are often sent to landfills because it's cheaper to dispose of them than to get them back onto shelves. Along with shopping less in general, perhaps consider donating an item to charity or offering it to a friend instead of returning it.

TAKING STOCK

Here's an example of a basic waste audit. Your family's audit may look a bit like this, but keep in mind that everyone and every family is different.

WHAT KIND OF WASTE?	IS THERE A WAY TO REDUCE IT?
KITCHEN GARBAGE 1. Paper napkins and paper towel 2. Food scraps 3. Individual snack packages	1. Use cloth napkins and rags (make your own out of old clothes!) 2. Compost 3. Buy larger packages or in bulk, or make some homemade snacks
KITCHEN RECYCLING 1. Glass jars 2. Produce packaging 3. Plastic bags	1. Use for storage or give to a local refill store 2. Choose unpackaged produce 3. Use reusable bags
BATHROOM GARBAGE AND RECYCLING 1. Tissues 2. Shampoo and conditioner bottles 3. Cotton balls	1. Switch to handkerchiefs (you can even make your own!) 2. Choose refills or bars 3. Use reusable cotton or flannel cloths (purchased or DIY)
OFFICE GARBAGE AND RECYCLING 1. Office paper 2. Construction paper 3. Used-up markers	1. Print on both sides of the paper 2. Use paper scraps for crafts and collages (make a scrap paper box for arts and crafts!) 3. Send used-up markers to a dedicated recycling program or drop-off facility

REFILL IT

Have you ever shopped at a refill store? These cool stores offer shoppers the chance to buy the products they want without any of the packaging waste. It's an awesome example of circular-economy shopping. Refill stores stock everything from personal care products (like soap, lotion and shampoo) to food (like pasta, beans and flour) in bulk. Refill stores often carry lots of other handy eco-friendly products too.

It's fun to explore refill stores because they have so many unique products. Some stores also offer online shopping and delivery.
MONKEYBUSINESSIMAGES/GETTY IMAGES

Here's how it works.

1. Bring your own clean containers, such as glass jars, cloth bags or reused plastic containers.
2. Go shopping! Some stores are self-serve, so you can fill your containers yourself. In other stores, the staff help customers fill their containers. (If you're using a heavy container like a glass jar, the weight of the jar is calculated and subtracted beforehand, so you only pay for the product itself.)
3. Your products are weighed, and the weight determines the price.
4. After you've used up your product, you clean the container and bring it back to the store for the next refill.
5. Refill stores often accept donations of containers. The next time you make spaghetti for dinner, you might be able to save and clean the pasta sauce jar to give to your local refill store. They would sanitize it and give it to customers who need extra jars.

If you and your family don't have a refill store nearby, there are lots of other eco-friendly options. Check out your local grocery store's bulk aisle, which is a similar concept. Some stores allow customers to bring their own containers. When buying packaged goods choose the largest package available or packaging that's easily recycled in your area. Farmers' markets are also wonderful

Of all the plastic produced in the world, an estimated 36 percent gets made into things like single-use packaging for food and beverage containers at the grocery store. Imagine how much plastic waste we could prevent by refill shopping!

Have you visited your local farmers' market? In addition to fresh produce, they commonly feature delicious baked goods, one-of-a-kind crafts, entertainment and so much more.
THOMAS BARWICK/GETTY IMAGES

places to shop with your own containers—you get to support local farmers and try delicious fruits and veggies. You may also have a low-waste grocery-delivery company in your area—check online to find out.

LOW-WASTE-IFY YOUR LUNCH

One of the best ways to keep your waste footprint small is to pack your school lunch. Some eco-friendly gear to get you started could include:

- A reusable lunch bag or container with dividers (bento box-style)
- A water bottle or travel mug
- Reusable snack containers or washable fabric snack bags
- Reusable cutlery and/or chopsticks
- A cloth napkin

Packing your own lunch doesn't just reduce waste. It also means that you can include your favorite foods and snacks! What do you like eating for lunch?
CLAUDIA TOTIR/GETTY IMAGES

It doesn't need to be fancy though—simple containers or cleaned and reused jars work perfectly. After you've gathered your low-waste lunch supplies, you might find it helpful to brainstorm some low-waste lunch ideas. Here are just a few:

- Unpackaged fruits and veggies, like carrot sticks, orange slices and apples
- Snacks purchased from the bulk section of your grocery or refill store, like trail mix, wasabi peas, roasted chickpeas, dried fruit, pretzels or treats
- Some simple-to-make foods, like edamame, homemade hummus or muffins

LOW-WASTE IN THE BATHROOM

If you and your family completed the waste audit at the beginning of this chapter, you might have noticed just how much waste is generated from products in the bathroom. Thankfully, there are tons of ways to switch up your bathroom routine so you can avoid and reduce waste. Here are some of the low-waste options you can find at eco-friendly stores:

- Toothpaste tabs or powder (check with your dentist first!)
- Bamboo toothbrush or a toothbrush with detachable refill heads
- Shampoo and conditioner bars or liquid refills
- Bar soap or liquid refills
- Solid body lotion or liquid refills
- Low-waste menstrual products, such as period underwear, cloth pads or menstrual cups
- Lip balm, deodorant, skin-care and hair products that are refillable or packaged in compostable containers
- Cloth handkerchiefs
- Toilet paper that comes in a cardboard box and is made from sustainable sources (like recycled paper)

Disposable plastic toothbrushes are often found in shoreline cleanups. Switching to low-waste versions can help reduce plastic waste.
OLGA PESHKOVA/GETTY IMAGES

It can be tricky (and expensive!) to switch over to *all* these options. Instead, try choosing one or two that might work for your family and see how it goes. What's even more fun is making some of these products yourself. Get inspired by one of these ideas:

- Gather your friends and have a lip-balm-making party with supplies like coconut oil, beeswax and shea butter. You can find tons of simple recipes online.
- Ask your teacher to teach the class how to sew cloth handkerchiefs.
- Take a soapmaking workshop online or in your community.

TRASH OR TREASURE?

When there's something we need, and we can't make, borrow or do without it, consider whether it can be bought used. Secondhand shopping is a huge industry. In 2021 the global market value of secondhand apparel was estimated to be US$96 billion.

Nada (a Spanish word that translates to "nothing") is a low-waste grocery store in Vancouver, BC. Friends and business partners Brianne Miller and Alison Carr opened the store to help people reduce waste. Shoppers use reusable containers for their groceries so they can avoid packaging. And since shoppers choose as much food as they want, they also reduce food waste.
NADA

You'll never know what sorts of hidden gems you'll find in used bookstores unless you go exploring. JORDAN LYE/GETTY IMAGES

Secondhand clothing stores can be so much fun. You may find a never-worn piece with the tags still on, or a cute vintage dress from your parents' or grandparents' era.
TREVOR WILLIAMS/GETTY IMAGES

Secondhand shopping also helps us avoid and reduce waste. By giving items a new home, we keep materials and resources out of the landfills and participate in the circular economy. Consider it a treasure hunt. A lot of the time, shopping secondhand means the item you find will be unique or more special than one you'd find at a big-box retailer.

Places you can shop for secondhand goods include the following:

Thrift stores or vintage boutiques: these can be very budget-friendly or very pricey, depending on the store

Online (with adult help, of course): this can include social media "shop and swap" groups or secondhand retailers

Local swaps with neighbors: examples include Little Free Libraries or clothing/toy swaps (check out "Stylish Swaps" in chapter 3 for more details)

OLD-FASHIONED SKILLS

When you read the words *knitting* and *baking bread*, do you think of things your grandmother might have done? Or do you think of things that young, eco-friendly activists do? They're both. Some of these supposedly old-fashioned skills are awesome ways to reduce waste—and they're pretty impressive life skills too.

Imagine being able to make a knitted scarf for your friend's birthday, or some homemade jam with the blueberries you picked in the summertime. Not only would you not have to buy something new from the store, but you could make things exactly as you like them while showing off your new talents.

Not sure where to learn a new skill? Your school may offer courses in food skills or textiles, or you may be able to take a class at a community center or online. You can also ask a grandparent or knowledgeable family member or friend.

Baking is a fantastic and delicious "old-fashioned" life skill. Other examples include cooking, sewing, quilting, woodworking, drying herbs and saving seeds.
PROSTOCK-STUDIO/SHUTTERSTOCK.COM

Living in a Low-Waste Family

Henry Barnes lives in Aurora, Ontario, with his mom, dad and brother. Together they do their best to be eco-friendly. For Henry and his brother, it's always been this way. "It feels normal," says Henry. "This is just how our family is, so I didn't know it was different until I got older." One of Henry's favorite things about living in a low-waste way is choosing food for his school lunches and snacks (including candy!) that his family buys packaging-free. He also likes shopping secondhand for things like toys, clothes and even Halloween costumes. Pretty much anything can be found secondhand, explains Henry, even though it sometimes takes a little longer to find something specific. As a family they also pick up litter, reuse things (like ice-cream cups for planting seedlings) and take action at the community level by attending protests. "I tell my friends about it, and they tell their parents, which is good for the planet," he says. "We're learning how to be kinder to the environment and only use what we really need and that's it."

Henry Barnes and his mother, Sarah Robertson-Barnes, live in a low-waste way.
SARAH ROBERTSON-BARNES

CHAPTER THREE

Let's Get Creative: Reuse

Reusing is next on the waste hierarchy, and it's arguably the most fun. This step is all about channeling your inner artist, because it's time to get creative. Sure, sometimes reusing just means, well, reusing—like when you reuse your lunch bag every day. But reusing can also mean repurposing, reimagining and repairing. The sky is the limit!

THE COLORFUL WORLD OF VISIBLE MENDING

So what happens when your favorite pair of jeans—the softest, comfiest, fit-like-a-glove pair of jeans—get a hole? There's no need to toss them aside when you can repair them. With visible mending, you can make clothing look even more beautiful than before—and perfectly personalized too.

Visible mending is a way to repair clothes (and other fabric-based items) in a way that highlights a garment's imperfections

What can you make with everyday so-called waste like empty beverage containers? With some craft supplies and imagination, the possibilities are endless!
ELVA ETIENNE/GETTY IMAGES

Do you know how to sew? You may learn how at school. If not, you could ask a knowledgeable friend or family member to teach you, or take classes. VGAJIC/GETTY IMAGES

rather than trying to conceal them. It's based on a Japanese stitching tradition called **sashiko**, which means "little stabs," and it has been used for hundreds of years. The result is a beautiful and unique piece of clothing that is also very strong. The best part is you don't even need a sewing machine to do it (although you certainly *can* use one). Visible mending can be done by hand with few materials—a needle and thread plus some fabric scraps. You can also learn skills such as sewing on a patch or a button and darning socks or sweaters.

NO SCRAP LEFT BEHIND

Once food is past its prime, there's actually a lot of ways to reuse it before it gets composted. And yes, composting is great, but take a moment to think about how much work and how many resources go into growing and making food—water, seeds, land, fertilizer and labor from farmers—not to mention the fuel for transporting it to us. Food production has a big environmental impact.

Sewing skills can be practical (like repairing holes in clothing) or creative (like hand embroidery) or both—like visible mending!
HOLLYHARRY/SHUTTERSTOCK.COM

27

Have this?	Try this!	Have this?	Try this!
OVERRIPE FRUIT	• Make a smoothie • Make a fruit crumble • Make a sauce, chutney or jam • Use it in baking (like bananas for banana bread) • Freeze it for later	**LEFTOVER COOKED POTATOES**	• Make shepherd's pie • Make fried potato cakes/balls
OVERRIPE VEGGIES	• Use in soups or stews • Make pesto from greens • Freeze herbs	**LEFTOVER COOKED RICE**	• Make fried rice • Make rice pudding • Add it to a soup
VEGGIE PEELS AND SCRAPS	• Make soup stock (and then use it or freeze it) • Use veggie dyes for clothing or Easter eggs	**LEFTOVER COOKED PASTA**	• Make a pasta salad • Add it to a soup
		PUMPKIN SEEDS (from carving jack-o'-lanterns)	• Roast them for a delicious snack
STALE BREAD	• Make bread pudding • Make croutons or breadcrumbs • Make panzanella (bread salad) or French onion soup	**LEFTOVER LIQUID FROM CANNED CHICKPEAS** (also known as aquafaba)	• Make vegan meringue • Use as an egg substitute in some vegan baking recipes

Computers, TVs, cell phones, printers and gaming equipment are common types of e-waste that we generate at home. PIC_STUDIO/GETTY IMAGES

GADGETS AND GIZMOS APLENTY

Electronics are a great example of waste that can be reused by repairing and refurbishing. Some waste is easier to dispose of than others. *E-waste* (short for "electronic waste") includes everything from computers and phones to batteries and fluorescent light bulbs. E-waste isn't safe to dispose of with regular garbage because it can leach toxic chemicals (such as heavy metals like lead or cadmium) when it breaks down. This is harmful to both the environment and human health.

The good news is that many components of e-waste, such as steel and copper, can be used again. But they need to be taken apart very carefully by people who are trained to do it, so that some parts can be reused and other parts can be disposed of safely. Sometimes an entire electronic item (like a computer) can be refurbished and used by someone else.

ELVAETIENNE/GETTY IMAGES

You can use food scraps such as green onions, celery, lettuce or leeks to grow more food. Leave the root intact and place it in water with the stem peeking out. Keep it watered, leave it in the sunlight (a windowsill is perfect) and watch it grow. Many food scraps can also be replanted in your garden, as long as the root structure is present.

Rethinking Food "Waste"

What happens when grocery stores, coffee shops, bakeries and restaurants have surplus food? A lot of the time it ends up in the compost—or, even worse, in the garbage. MealCare is a nonprofit organization led by university students that is working to change that. The students coordinate with local donors (such as restaurants and grocery stores) and divert their surplus food to places that need it, like homeless shelters and youth shelters.

Rahmah Ikhlas is president of the University of Ottawa chapter. As an immigrant to Canada, she was surprised to learn that people were going hungry in a wealthy country. She wanted to make a difference, so she started volunteering at MealCare. "Food waste is very easy to ignore in our society," she says. "But it's important to observe what can be salvaged and be mindful of all the possibilities of so-called waste!"

Jessica Seifried is co-president of the University of Guelph chapter. Along with her fellow volunteers, she brainstormed a list of actions we can take at home to reduce food waste.

MealCare volunteers carefully plan meals and prepare food.
MYA CITRIGNO

- Take what you'll eat and eat what you take.
- Pack your own lunch (so you'll choose foods you enjoy and will eat them).
- Fight against the stigma of imperfect-looking produce. Choose and use veggies and fruit that might not be 100 percent beautiful.
- Learn where your food comes from.
- Challenge your family to come up with the tastiest meal you can using leftovers.

One key thing Rahmah and Jessica want people to know is that there's a difference between true food waste (which cannot be consumed) and surplus food. The food donated through MealCare is good, nutritious food—definitely *not* garbage!

Four-Blade Wrap

Flat-Object Wrap

① ①

② ②

③ ③

④ ④

SINGULAR FACT/SHUTTERSTOCK.COM

Like other forms of garbage, e-waste doesn't always end up where it should. Sometimes it is sent overseas to illegal dumping sites or taken apart by people in an unsafe way that puts their health at risk. Globally about 59 million tons (53.6 million tonnes) of e-waste were generated in 2019 alone.

We can help minimize e-waste by recycling our electronics correctly. Do an online search to find electronic recycling options where you live, or see if the electronic manufacturer has a take-back program. You might even be able to donate old electronics that still work to local charities. But remember to delete your information on any old electronics first! When it's time to buy new electronics, you can buy a refurbished model.

IT'S A WRAP

Happy holidays! According to the group Zero Waste Canada, 600,759 tons (545,000 tonnes) of waste from gift-wrapping supplies is generated every year. And we use 6 million rolls of tape! No matter which holidays you and your family celebrate, it can be easy and fun to wrap gifts in a low-waste way that also looks great. All you need are some repurposed materials and a bit of imagination.

Furoshiki are traditional Japanese cloths used for wrapping items. (The term refers to both the fabric and the practice of wrapping.) They're a perfect way to wrap gifts with reusable materials. Don't worry—you don't need special cloths. Consider using these materials:

- Vintage scarves, tea towels, cloth napkins or handkerchiefs (they can often be found at thrift stores for a really great price)
- Out-of-date maps, flyers or calendars
- Brown packing paper from deliveries (kraft paper)
- Newspaper (the comic section is especially fun to wrap with)
- Old magazines

Wrapping hard-to-wrap gifts is so much easier with cloth than paper—and the result is so pretty!
ROSITA RUTKAUSKIENE / EYEEM/GETTY IMAGES

- A paper bag, cloth bag or burlap sack
- A glass jar
- An old shoebox

Sometimes you can make the wrapping part of the gift itself—you could wrap the item in a knitted scarf, for example.

STYLISH SWAPS

Looking for an excuse to have a party...while also practicing reusing? Why not host a clothing swap with your friends? It's a great idea for so many reasons. With a clothing swap, you can:

- Keep clothing out of the landfill
- Find some new stylish pieces—for free
- Try out some new trends that you've never worn before
- Share your passion for low-waste living with others

Ready to swap? Here's how to get started:
- Make sure you have an adult attending to help organize and supervise.
- Choose a location, whether it's in someone's backyard or inside at someone's house.
- Pick a date and invite your friends! Classmates, siblings, neighbors, your soccer team...the list goes on. It's great to get a diverse group of people with lots of different sizes. That way, everyone can find something that fits them.
- Let people know to bring clean used clothes that are in good condition to pass along to others. It's also a good idea to encourage guests to contribute fairly if they will be taking lots of items home with them.
- Set up the space with bins, tables, hangers and racks for people to place their clothing items. Label areas so people know where to drop off their old clothes and where to browse for new clothes. You can sort things by type or size or both.

You can add some fun finishing touches to your wrapped gift. Consider reused ribbon, twine, natural materials (like holly, pine cones, evergreen boughs or dried leaves/flowers) or an upcycled gift tag.
ARTISTGNDPHOTOGRAPHY/GETTY IMAGES

Clothing swaps are so fun! Your class or school could organize one—consider asking your teacher. TARTANPARTY/SHUTTERSTOCK.COM

Get to know the local repairing pros in your area. Repairing something is often much more cost-effective (and way kinder to the planet) than rebuying something. Encourage the adults in your household to take shoes to a cobbler, clothes to a tailor and antiques or furniture to restoration professionals.

Caring for our clothes properly can make them last longer. Be sure to follow the instructions on the tag, like washing in cold water, hanging to dry and washing bright colors separately from light colors. HOLLYHARRY/SHUTTERSTOCK.COM

- Remember to have a place for people to change. Maybe it's a bathroom, or maybe it's an outdoor "fitting room" that you create with curtains.
- Include a mirror so people can see themselves in the clothes they're trying on.
- If you like, provide some snacks and refreshments to enjoy with your guests, and play some music.
- Donate leftover items to local charities (more on that in the next section).

Remember, a clothing swap is just one kind of swap party. You can do the same with books, toys, sports equipment, Halloween costumes or other items.

PASS IT ON

We know it's important to think about where items will end up after we toss them in the recycling or garbage—but what about after we toss them in a donation pile? Not everything we donate ends up in the hands of those who could really use it.

We tend to donate way more clothes than what is truly needed locally. Only about 20 to 25 percent is reused or resold in our communities. If you've caught the decluttering bug, be mindful with the items you no longer want. Rather than simply dropping off items at a thrift store, think about how to get them to people who want them. Here are some ideas:

- Whenever possible, repair or **upcycle** damaged items to extend their life spans. Then do your best to clean your items before donating them, to make them as attractive as possible.
- Ask your friends or family members if they want something.
- Host a clothing swap (see page 31) or garage sale.
- With help from an adult, post an item online for sale or for free (such as in a neighborhood "shop and swap" group on social media).

- Bring items to a consignment shop. These stores carefully vet items to ensure that there's a market for them before accepting them.
- Donate items to a specific charitable cause by researching nonprofits beforehand with help from an adult.

Wondering what you might be able to donate to whom? Check out these ideas:

- Mascara wands to wildlife rescue centers (to clean and brush small animals)
- Wire clothing hangers to dry cleaners
- Toiletries and bras to women's shelters
- Pet supplies or old towels to animal shelters
- Eyeglasses to optometrists, where they are then donated to those in need
- Food, menstrual products and diapers to food banks
- Warm clothing, blankets and household goods to homeless shelters

Remember, always double-check with a charity or organization first to find out if they're currently accepting donations. It might take a little extra time, but it will ensure that your old items end up exactly where they need to be so they can be reused by others.

If your old clothing isn't in a wearable condition, you may be able to bring it to a textile-recycling drop-off location rather than trying to donate it. Or you can turn it into rags or make patches for other pieces of clothing.
FG TRADE/GETTY IMAGES

Consider chatting with some neighbors to see if they want to join in on a block-wide garage sale. That way everyone can take part.
AJ_WATT/GETTY IMAGES

CHAPTER FOUR

All's Well That Ends Well: Recycle and Rot

Some communities have curbside recycling pickup. People sort their recycling into bins and then take the bins out to the curb for big recycling trucks to pick up, as seen here. RYASICK/GETTY IMAGES

As expert low-wasters, we now know that it's always best to follow the first steps on the waste hierarchy (avoid, reduce and reuse) before the lower steps (recycle and rot). As strange as it sounds at first, we want to have to recycle and compost *less,* not more, because that means we've done a better job of avoiding, reducing and reusing. However, we still do need to learn how to do these final steps correctly.

Let's start with learning to be recycling rock stars. As it turns out, it's a bit more complicated than you might have originally thought. Even the adults in your life might be doing parts of it wrong. (But now *you* can teach *them* how to do it properly!)

NO WISH-CYCLING ALLOWED!

Wish-cycling is a term for tossing something into the recycling bin and hoping it will be recycled, even though it probably won't be.

Chances are there's at least one item you and your family accidentally wish-cycle. As we learn more about our recycling system and what can be recycled where we live, we can improve our own recycling habits and help others do the same. RAWPIXEL/GETTY IMAGES

Most of us have done this at some point, whether it's a potato-chip bag or plastic cutlery, both of which are typically not recyclable. But putting things in the recycling bin that can't be recycled is unhelpful, and it just creates more work for the people who work at recycling depots. Sometimes it can even be hazardous—plastic bags, for example, which are often not accepted in curbside recycling programs, could clog up machinery. So how do you avoid wish-cycling? Easy. Do your research!

DO YOUR RESEARCH

Being a recycling pro starts with learning about your municipality's recycling system. That's because every system is so different

Aluminum is a recycling rock star! Deemed "infinitely recyclable," aluminum can be recycled into new cans and be back on grocery store shelves in six weeks. It takes 95 percent less energy to make a can from recycled aluminum than using new materials. According to the Aluminum Association, 75 percent of the aluminum produced in the United States is still in use.

Does your community have a plastic-packaging takeback program? In some areas customers can collect and return plastic packaging (like stand-up pouches, zipper-lock bags and potato-chip bags) to designated drop-off locations. This plastic may not be technically *recyclable*, but it might be *returnable*. This means that the plastic may be studied so people can learn how to recycle it. It might also be recovered and processed into fuel.

that it's hard to give advice that works for *every* area. What might be recyclable in one area isn't recyclable in another. Some rural areas do not have curbside pickup. It's time to put on your detective hat and research your city or town's recycling system.

- What kinds of items are accepted by your curbside recycling program (if you have one)? What needs to be taken to a recycling depot?
- Where do specialty items like batteries or aerosol containers go?
- For items that are not recyclable, does your city offer a takeback program? For example, can you return chip bags or snack packaging somewhere, or do they go in the trash?
- Is there anything you should do to the items? For example, should you flatten cereal and tissue boxes? Can items be bagged together?

Now that you know more about your community's recycling program, you might want to print off or write down a list and put it on the fridge or in another area of your home where your family will see it, so everyone can refer to it!

AS EASY AS ONE, TWO, THREE

Did you know that there are different types of plastics? Often (but not always!) you can find out the type of plastic by reading the number on the item's resin code. Those little numbers in the middle of the arrows don't guarantee that an item is recyclable. All they tell you is what kind of material it is. Some types of plastic are commonly recyclable, some are not commonly recyclable and some are in the middle.

But wait! Other materials have recycling codes too. In your recycling journey you might come across ones such as PAP-22 (paper) or GL-70 (glass).

Unfortunately, just because a code indicates an item is typically recyclable doesn't mean it is actually accepted for recycling. For example, plastic straws that are made out of #5 plastic are rarely accepted for recycling, even if a municipality accepts other #5 items.

If you're wondering where **biodegradable** plastics fit in, you're not alone. Lots of people these days are curious about plant-based **bioplastics** or plastics labeled *biodegradable*. You might have seen them as takeout-food containers or cups. Unfortunately, some bioplastics are not biodegradable. And bioplastics/biodegradable plastics are rarely accepted in typical recycling programs or composting programs. Biodegradable plastics often require the high temperatures of industrial composters to break down, and many cities don't have access to those composters. Those plastics likely won't break down in nature either. This is why bringing our reusables when we're out and about is important!

Big pieces of plastic in the environment tend to break down into smaller and smaller bits, like these. Eventually they turn into microplastics, which are about the size of sesame seeds or even smaller. DOBLE-D/GETTY IMAGES

	NAME	EXAMPLE	RECYCLABLE?
♳ PET	PETE/PET (polyethylene terephthalate)	BEVERAGE BOTTLE	Typically accepted
♴ HDPE	HDPE (high-density polyethylene)	MILK JUG	Typically accepted
♵ PVC	PVC (polyvinyl chloride)	PIPING	Less likely to be accepted
♶ LDPE	LDPE (low-density polyethylene)	SHOPPING BAG	Less likely to be accepted
♷ PP	PP (polypropylene)	VITAMIN BOTTLE	Sometimes accepted
♸ PS	PS (polystyrene)	FOAM TAKEOUT CONTAINER	Less likely to be accepted
♹ OTHER	Other	SAFETY GLASSES	Less likely to be accepted

KEEP IT CLEAN

So you're not wish-cycling and you know what's recyclable in your area. What now? Before your recycling is sent off to the depot, it's important to help prevent **recycling contamination** by making sure your items are clean. Here are some tips:

Cleaning containers properly is important when we recycle. It's also super important when we intend to reuse materials, like glass jars. Depending on what we're using the jars for, they can be washed with hot soapy water or even sterilized (with the help of an adult).
PEANGDAO/GETTY IMAGES

Sort your materials properly. In some municipalities there is only one recycling bin per household, but many have several different kinds, for plastic, paper, aluminum and so on.

Remove grease, such as the oily bottom of a pizza box (which may be composted). Yes, that means you should carefully tear or cut apart boxes so as much can be salvaged as possible.

Rinse containers. Items that are wet or dirty can't be recycled. If they are added to the recycling, other items can get wet and dirty too, and then they can't be recycled either.

FROM SCRAPS TO SOIL

Here we are, at the final step of the waste hierarchy. To recap, we first learned how to avoid and reduce, and then how to reuse (including repairing, reimagining and refurbishing). *Rot* typically gets grouped with *recycle* and refers to the magic of composting. Well, it's not really magic, but it *is* pretty amazing!

Composting is the process by which organic material (whether it's your leftover sandwich or the fallen autumn leaves in your backyard) is broken down by microorganisms (like bacteria and fungi) and other decomposers (like earthworms). The finished product is called compost or **humus** (no, not hummus, the delicious dip!). Humus makes soil nutrient-rich and able to grow new things. This humus is so important that farmers sometimes refer to it as "black gold."

For composting to happen, you need the following elements:

- Water
- Air (which contains oxygen)
- Organic matter (which includes "browns" and "greens")

If we think back to what we learned about landfills, this explains why food and other organic matter don't break down properly in landfills—they don't receive all the things they need for composting to occur, like air.

In composting lingo, "browns" are carbon-rich organic materials such as dried leaves, twigs and shredded newspaper. "Greens" are nitrogen-rich organic materials such as fresh grass clippings and food scraps. Not all organic matter belongs in the compost though—some things that should never be composted include human and pet bodily waste, cat litter and any diseased or invasive plants.

Do you compost? An estimated 76 percent of households in Canada do, and the number seems to be increasing. That's pretty impressive! RENATA ANGERAMI/GETTY IMAGES

Compost does best if it is watered and turned or stirred. This helps the air and water reach all the helpful microorganisms. It also helps speed up the composting process so the humus will mature more quickly. The process of composting produces heat, but it doesn't get too hot in a home-based compost system. As we learned, that's why biodegradable plastics don't tend to break down in regular composting environments or in nature. They need higher temperatures, like those created by industrial composters.

Compost is a great example of a food chain. We eat food, and our leftover food is eaten by microorganisms and decomposers, which then create nutrient-rich compost so we can grow more food. It might be an efficient scientific process, but it sure feels magical!

GETTING STARTED WITH COMPOSTING

Interested in composting? Here are a few different ways to get started:

Municipal composting programs. Your municipality may have a composting program where you save food scraps from your kitchen and they get picked up or dropped off for the city to compost. If so, carefully read your municipality's instructions for how to line your food-scrap bin and what can be included in it. You may or may not be able to include things like paper towel, eggshells, dairy, used tea bags, and meat, bones and seafood. (Compostable plastics and plastic bags are typically not allowed, but it's good to double-check just in case.)

At-home outdoor composting. If you have a yard, you may be able to carry out the composting process yourself with a garden composter purchased through your city. You can put various food scraps in it, along with garden waste. You may not wish to include items that attract pests and

We can collect our kitchen food scraps in containers like these before adding them to our compost. JENNY DETTRICK/GETTY IMAGES

rodents, like dairy, grease, meat, bones and seafood. Both "browns" and "greens" are needed (sometimes in layers), and as you just learned, you probably want to turn or stir the compost. The great thing is that the process creates beautiful humus you can use to nourish your home garden. Check out your community's recycling or waste-management website for materials, instructions and resources.

At-home indoor composting. It's possible to compost at home even if you don't have a yard and even if you live in a condo or apartment building. One really cool option is called *vermicomposting*, and it involves worms (yes, really!). In this process, special worms in well-ventilated containers help break down food scraps and other compostable materials.

A Low-Waste Activist

Mason volunteers in his community on a regular basis.
SHANNA KANUKA

Think kids can't make a difference? Think again! Mason Vander Ploeg is a high school student from Langley, British Columbia, who has been helping fight plastic pollution since he was nine years old. He was inspired by visiting the Vancouver Aquarium and the ocean when he was young. In addition to recycling and packing waste-free lunches, Mason regularly helps with and organizes shoreline cleanups and volunteers with local environmental organizations, including the Nicomekl Salmon Hatchery. He also takes part in classroom education, sharing his passion for the ocean with students in younger grades.

If you want to get involved too, consider writing to companies and politicians, as well as volunteering in your own community. "Don't be discouraged!" says Mason. "Start slowly and take little steps...You're not too young for your voice to be heard. Just start somewhere!"

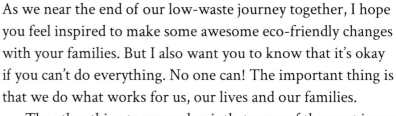

BEYOND THE WASTE HIERARCHY

As we near the end of our low-waste journey together, I hope you feel inspired to make some awesome eco-friendly changes with your families. But I also want you to know that it's okay if you can't do everything. No one can! The important thing is that we do what works for us, our lives and our families.

The other thing to remember is that some of the most important work we can do as individuals is to push for changes that make reducing waste easier for everyone and benefit the community as a whole. As individuals we have a lot of responsibility and power, but so do governments and corporations. And while our individual and household waste matters, the actions of governments and corporations have a much bigger impact on the environment. We need to hold them accountable for the waste they create and the pollution they emit. And yes, here too kids and teens can make things better!

What does low-waste activism look like? Here are some ideas to help inspire you:

Getting involved in our communities can be a fun and rewarding experience. You can start small, with one project you feel excited about. FILIPPOBACCI/GETTY IMAGES

- Start a "green team" or environmental club at school.
- Help your school go low-waste by composting food scraps and improving its recycling programs.
- With your school or friends, organize a litter pickup or shoreline cleanup.
- Attend your town council meetings and share your thoughts about things such as your community's waste-reduction goals or composting strategy.
- Write to your local politicians and newspapers about issues you are passionate about, such as community-wide strategies to reduce single-use plastics.
- Encourage your school to host a book/toy/clothing swap.
- Learn where your local recycling and garbage goes. Ask your school to do a field trip to your local landfill, recycling depot or repair café.

- Have a low-waste skill like mending or seed saving? Help teach it to others.
- Research environmental groups and nonprofits near you and reach out to get involved and volunteer.
- Find and connect with like-minded kids who share your passion for low-waste living.

It's exciting to see how much amazing work is being done all over the world to promote a circular economy and help reduce waste in creative ways. We can all make a difference together!

These kids are taking part in a shoreline cleanup. You may be able to get involved in a shoreline cleanup, litter pickup or nature-restoration project near you. SOLSTOCK/GETTY IMAGES

Resources

Print

Delisle, Raina. *Fashion Forward: Striving for Sustainable Style.* Orca Book Publishers, 2022.

Elton, Sarah. *Starting from Scratch: What You Should Know about Food and Cooking.* Owlkids Books Inc., 2014.

Klein, Naomi, and Rebecca Stefoff. *How to Change Everything: The Young Human's Guide to Protecting the Planet and Each Other.* Puffin Canada, 2021.

Mulder, Michelle. *Trash Talk: Moving Toward a Zero-Waste World.* Orca Book Publishers, 2015.

Scheunemann, Pam. *Trash to Treasure: A Kid's Upcycling Guide to Crafts.* Mighty Media Junior Readers, 2013.

Tate, Nikki. *Better Together: Creating Community in an Uncertain World.* Orca Book Publishers, 2018.

Online

David Suzuki Foundation: davidsuzuki.org

Environmental Defence: environmentaldefence.ca

Love Food Hate Waste: lovefoodhatewaste.com

Ocean Wise: ocean.org

Repair Café: repaircafe.org/en

Story of Stuff Project: storyofstuff.org

Zero Waste Canada: zerowastecanada.ca

Zero Waste International Alliance: zwia.org

Links to external resources are for personal and/or educational use only and are provided in good faith without any express or implied warranty. There is no guarantee given as to the accuracy or currency of any individual item. The author and publisher provide links as a service to readers. This does not imply any endorsement by the author or publisher of any of the content accessed through these links.

Glossary

biodegradable—able to break down naturally in a way that is not harmful to the environment

bioplastics—plastics derived from plants (rather than from petroleum)

circular economy—an economic system in which waste is viewed as a raw material. It's reduced and, whenever possible, materials are repurposed, repaired or reused rather than disposed of; called such because it moves in a circular line

closed loop—a way of designing and producing goods with the goal of keeping them in the economy for as long as possible

compost—the breaking down of organic material by microorganisms and other decomposers to create nutrient-rich humus (also sometimes referred to as *compost*)

consumerist—relating to a way of life that values buying and owning things

environmental racism—discrimination in environmental policies and decision-making based on race, particularly in terms of which people end up negatively affected by environmental problems like pollution and climate change

e-waste—electronic waste, such as printers, cell phones and computer cords

fossil fuels—nonrenewable fuels (materials used to produce energy) such as coal, oil and natural gas that are formed over millions of years by plant or animal remains

furoshiki—traditional Japanese cloths used for wrapping items

greenhouse gas—a gas that traps heat in the earth's atmosphere, such as carbon dioxide and methane

humus—the end product of composting, also known as *mature compost*

industrialized—having lots of businesses and factories for producing things

landfills—specialized places where large amounts of garbage are placed and managed

linear economy—an economic system in which resources are taken from the earth, made into products and then disposed of once people are done using them; called such because it moves in a straight line through the various steps of the supply chain

microplastics—tiny plastic pieces (less than five millimeters long) that pollute land and water

recycling contamination—nonrecyclable materials that end up in the recycling stream, or recyclable materials that become unusable for various reasons (such as a bit of food still in a container)

refill—in regard to low-waste living, to fill a container again so it can be used rather than getting a new container (refill shopping is part of the circular economy)

resources—materials or possessions that are valuable and useful

sashiko—a Japanese stitching tradition, which translates to "little stabs," upon which visible mending is based

upcycled—recycled in a way that gives the new item greater value than the original item

vermicomposting—a composting method that uses worms to facilitate the process

visible mending—a way to repair clothes (and other fabric-based items) in a way that highlights a garment's imperfections rather than trying to conceal them, based on the Japanese stitching tradition called *sashiko*

waste audit—a process through which you organize, catalog and track the waste you produce in order to figure out how to reduce it

waste hierarchy—a tool that looks like an upside-down pyramid and ranks ways to use and dispose of things, from most preferred to least preferred, reminding us of all the ways we can reduce waste

waterways—navigable bodies of water

zero waste—a philosophy and a movement with the goal of reducing waste and conserving resources

Index

Page numbers in **bold** indicate an image caption.

Acknowledgments

I would first like to acknowledge that the lands upon which I live and work are the unceded Traditional Coast Salish Lands of the Squamish (Sḵwx̱wú7mesh Úxwumixw), Tsleil-Waututh (səl̓ilw̓ətaʔɬ) and Musqueam (xʷməθkʷəy̓əm) Nations.

I am honored to have had the opportunity to write this book. Thank you to Orca Book Publishers and my wonderful editor, Kirstie Hudson, for taking a chance on a new author and for all of your help making this book a reality.

My utmost gratitude goes to everyone I interviewed and consulted when researching and writing this book. Thank you to my good friend, expert reader and fellow low-waste mom, Sarah Robertson-Barnes. My heartfelt appreciation goes to those involved in Ban the Bottle and/or Re-use for Good at Simon Fraser University (including but not limited to Mireta Strandberg-Salmon, Elaina Buenaventura, Antonia Kowalewski, Serena Bains and Teghan Acres); those involved in MealCare (including but not limited to Milton Calderon, Rahmah Ikhlas and Jessica Seifried); Mason Vander Ploeg and Shanna Kanuka; Henry Barnes; and Brianne Miller for their work, as well as for sharing their experiences and expertise for this book.

Finally, thank you to my family for their ongoing support when I was writing this book, from childcare to cooking to cheering me on. Without your help this book would simply not exist.

Thank you, everyone!

LEAH PAYNE is a writer and editor. She holds a bachelor's degree in communication from Simon Fraser University and a master's degree in library and information studies from the University of British Columbia. Leah lives with her family in Vancouver, British Columbia. As a mother, she is passionate about sustainability and loves hearing the incredible stories of young environmentalists working to make the world a better place. *Less Is More* is her first book.